To my beloved children

Mimoza, Blinera, Liria, Andi

ISBN: 978-91-78-517 96-1

© Myrvete Osmani 2020

Förlag: BoD – Books on Demand, Stockholm, Sverige

Tryck: BoD – Books on Demand, Norderstedt, Tyskland

Editor: Naime Beqiraj

Translator: Fadil Bajrar

Time

We cry, because the time is over us

We cry, because life is our crying,

Smile and warmth

sun keeps for itself

Between the fingers of tired hands

We penetrate our smiles

Because time

Will mysteriously steal our laughs.

Say at Least One Word

My silence

which rest in my bosom

my untold stories are shouts

of white nights,

tonight, me and my word, we only have

pain and suffer

O my silence,

you left illuminated only the path to my grave

flickering

as an old leaflet

under the open shadow of the fig tree

The only epitaph inside the railing

of my flower garden

say at least one word

Sunday

Every Sunday

when the streets without the two of us

quietly sleep,

let the night cover them incomprehensibly

with all the longing

and wound that hurts.

Me and the Moon

When I cry only moon feels me

in her gaze

I become tears and hang on stars' eyelids

and I never stop

I've traveled thousands of years to reach you

and be killed by you,

or, at least, to wound me

But keep quiet. Keep quiet like night

because the night is a mystery

as you have been and will remain forever

Give Me Memories

Tonight I'm running away from you

without saying a word,

the snow

is falling again

Let me take the memories

with me,

to write the verses

and to turn them into a song

even this time

Saturday

Saturday reminds me of my maidenhood

the silent tomb

at the end of a lawn

There lies tenderness and begins the forest

overwhelmed by spring fowls

and birds

Morning nightmares

wake up with the dreams that are being killed

And again together

me and you, my maidenhood.

My World

Come on, my world, I will not part with you

even when pieces of a broken heart

drop like rain

Leaning against my chest

you feel lonely

and you are sobbing in silence

my wintry mad one

Winds blow, cyclones explode

statues fall,

let them fall, let they keep falling

I still hold you

In my chest.

Free Verse of My Soul

I do not put a period or a comma in my verse

let it be completely free,

beyond borders, braces

let it overtake the blue shores

without chains

Between the verses I want to be a flying bird

without a question mark and whys

without any answer

I will put a question mark as a spear

in the bow of my soul

because I want my verse to be naked

and loose

like freedom itself.

A Solo with Flowers

Through a wide lawn

the smell of flowers and green grass is felt

The Gods came down at night

and they fondle their lovers

The sounds of the wind are playing with flowers

a solo with stunning notes

Tonight

Tonight I want to raise a toast

for you

dear

In the dark field of the night

I will light a candle

I'll take

winds

as a soul pawn

I don't want this flame that brightens

your path to me to go out

Only One Single Moment

I feel everywhere

your fragrance this spring

dear

The sky casts your glance

at me

Flower petals

resemble your skin

and your scent

This light breeze

caresses me like your hand

Dear, I long

to live a moment

only a single moment with You

The poor would be richer

only in a kingdom

that lives with love

Kiss Me

Kiss me with your dry lips

kiss me till the morning

quench my thirst

don't let me die

Kiss me with your dry lips kiss me

and don't go away

Take me there

where

Gods made love

Memories

I never wanted to hurt you

This is a grey world my friend
your words are buzzing in my ears

Let the memories remain memories
but at least we should not hurt them
we should not let them smell of sadness

Simply, sing your song as best as You can
I can hear it from afar
to grab any harp, or curse

I want to rest, I want to be left alone
But at least, not to cry anymore

I'm Coming Back

I'm coming back

in my dreams tonight

Let their anxieties

judge me!

Let them come to the funeral

dumb warriors

the defeated and looters

Broken chariots

let them drag

Troy crumbled in flames

from the unfaithful ones

but I will not crumble

nor burn

Mournful Blessing

I do not forget that moment

as I have fled

how I've been crying

on an abandoned road

In my hands I held dangling

million dreams as pawn

I was drowning my tears

in the islands of the soul

and I continued mournfully

With the beggars from the neighborhood

of oblivion

we squeezed and killed

sad sensations

Day and night

were divided by barbed borders

the night has swallowed bloody coughs

Tired caravan

over worn out shoes

miles away

followed by stinking smoke of smog

Endless procession

to countless blessings

went and came back grey-haired

from death to death

mournfully

The Goddess

She, a beautiful Helen

A goddess

In the middle of rustling leaves in the wind of time

Following the sounds of the steps

Above the shallow waters of the river

She remains being a Helen

Even when the winds blow

When rain hit the roofs

When portraits wrinkle

In his eyes

In the grey retinas

She will remain the goddess

Even when all the flowers will turn gray in her
crown of hair

When they turn into a weak bird

And when they fly away

Following the winds

When seasons of life change

Years won't change you

Don't Flirt Tonight

You are full of flirt

Even when I say

Don't flirt tonight

But let your heart beat for me

If you can

Follow the smell of jasmines

Go down to the garden

And through the navel of the river

Sail with the language of your soul

The land is laying down

The land is a woman

That dares

Hide your lust under the skin

Wrap and unwrap

Sneakily the entire body

Because butterflies that come out of your eyes

Kiss my belly

Half with Traces

Tonight I'll drink only two halfway filled glasses

Two halfway filled glasses with rum

and I do dare to talk to you

and to talk even to myself

Only from this engraving

where moon casts its beams

and it breaks into a blue mirror

during twelve months of the year

for every night

during twelve months of the year

for every day

As I break

Far away from your eyes

And I fall down

In the ashy green lawns

Tonight I am drinking two halfway filled glasses

And a glass full of rum

Exhausted from love

With open arms I hit the road

The way to you is untrodden

Or well-trodden path

Full of traces

To Warm You Up

I'm your built castle

With stones of great love

I am your river with gilded water

When you come to wash your face because of the
heat

I am a parched wood in a fireplace

Burned to warm you up

When it's cold

I am the best thing that can happen to you

Just be my life for me

rain and sun, a blessed word

Lullaby of Loneliness

How scary is this road

How unfamiliar this spirit is

I don't understand the drowsiness of the night's
eyes

Why they look at me so sadly

I am throwing snowballs

At a beggar who waits outside the door in the late
hour

Although it's a yellow beginning of autumn

I have a very little fruit in the basket

Still Life

I'm waiting for you again

Among the fishermen by a lake without water

To catch dead fish

For a new plague

In the new century

To collect dead butterflies

Through the burned cobs

Only for the stinking mouths

Of big fish

Love Me As Much As I Love You

I'm wandering through the alleys of my town

Tonight I'll be waiting for you

Even if I accidentally meet you

Because I see your reflection in my dream

Near the beautiful road under silver clouds

The moon washes its face on the hill

With a constant autumn rain

Tearing the plump fruits

Quinces, forbidden apples color of sin

There are shadows that are frightening the silence

To awaken a life between us

We are drinking the pollen of the love

Without hurry without worry

May our tongues

Burn out of sweetness

O Lord, bless our innocence

And every true love

So, love me, as much as I love you

May our tongues

Burn out of sweetness

Even Love Dies

Breath into a loop

My tonight's nightmare

Why should you be that

What am I to do with your age

That have turned into a greedy raven

And eats dogs' flesh and everything else

It's too late tonight to go

To your path

I didn't know but even love dies

Promises

Someday I will die

Without realizing how

Why should

It be you

Let Me Wish You Luck

I would like to buy you a jacket with emerald
buttons

To dress you with it tonight

And to drink a beer

Then having another one

To get drunk

And to make love once in a year

Then to go out with an iron frame

Like abandoned birds

You would slip

Your rough hands

Through my body under my red dress

And kiss my neck

Adorned with silver necklaces

My baritone

If you'd sing me a song

And to slow down death

To return to my garden

Shelter

When I'm gone

One part of your sun

Will be my shelter

Half of your lawn under my feet, its green grass

Half-moon of the full moon at the late night

That grey gold hair of your hair

When I'm gone

Half of your soul

Half of your kiss

Half of your life

Half of your death

When I'm gone

When you will not be my full half

Don't talk to me

You Will Remember Me

You will remember me

As the evening undresses in front of the eyes

And the night lasts a thousand years

And the moon stays above the clouds

You will remember me

When loneliness as a wet shirt

Sticks to your body, will irritate you

And luck will never

Strike you again

You will remember me

With Dilemma

Poets laugh with their pain

They are a little unfair to themselves

They are a bit of cheaters

But they never cheat the others

Endless

You are my rain, autumn with ripe fruits

Flock of butterflies, oh, at the end of the flower
garden

You are a rose with a face of light

On the tip of red hair

Light of my face, my smiling lips

You are my path to the light that will show me

What means for love

To pick you up and taste you

This Time With My Heart

How does this moon look at me tonight

How sad the moon looks at me tonight

It enters between concrete pillars

Through ruins of cairns particles of light

To see my eyes

Hair bangs cut with scissors made of fingers

Hands

Where I want to throw

A grain of grapes with heart

This dumb night is silent

Over insect noises I am dying

Drunk insects covered by fog

With writhing dust

O God

What hungry panthers on the sandbank

Howling like dogs

With coppered faces inside boxes

This time with my heart I started out of the square

God is shaking a tree

This time he is doing it completely different

Far Away from Sister

This season of flowering is coming back this time

As a cold pelerine when it plays late at night

And as if with fingers touches my gray hair

We see each other once a year

Or once in four years

My brother, sister

My brother

God!

I prepared mulberry tea tonight

Because of yearning I talk to myself and to you

And I am drinking

I am getting drunk in silence

Like Ships

Lightly, lightly they sail

They are back to the edge of the pain

To take the lost destinies

Through the streets

From the collapsed time of rabid and despicable

Cursing

They are leaving in a hurry and strongly

Far from the shadow of the tree

With broken branches

Even if the sun will no longer warm them in the
promised land

Both young and old are leaving

On the branches of plum, on the roots of the red
dogwood

To eat creatures' lives

Every night, pilgrims are praying in the temple of
God,

In silent crying praying for peace

They are writing their names on white oaks,

And wearing skin of butchered sheep

They give meat in the name of God

Maybe they will have happy trails

They want

They give away everything they have

In a poor home

They only drag their bones and souls with them

As if scared they are running away from their sun

Slightly they go

O God

Destroy All Loopholes

For the fatherland to die in our hands

Is more than a shame

Because the fatherland never dies in the hands of
the enemy

If you get killed by your son

That's not forgivable by God

That's an open wound

It will never heal

If you betray salt and bread,

The waters that ran through fatherland's veins

That you drank

Your blood will turn into yellowish water

If the fatherland dies in your hands

It is more than a shame

It is more than unforgivable death

From those dead and those alive

How

How can I continue my journey today in this big
city?

where the sun goes out a bit to wash its eyes with
mixed mist

in aluminum dust without air

and flees furiously as if afraid to forgive the light

and maybe I need to run away too

It's better to be hated by bad ones than good ones

but it'd be much better

if I could hide even from myself in the mirror

and not to see my eyes burning at the wonders on
the road

and from the evil that I've seen in the light

I'd better run away

or with shouts to topple down the night to the
ground

and the day to be cleaner

and to see with eyes that has no fear

while I run around to find myself

rom within it doesn't seem to me short at all.

Days Quickly Flying

Let them run away from my trembling hand
Water did not drip in my jug
To moisten my sore lips
When I had feverish heat all day long,
As the dawn lights up the sky with no moon and
stars

I am alone without you

Let them go away even this autumn

and this whole year between teeth as winter times

and me as an exhausted old sheep

to bleat in green fields unseared by the sun

To fall in love with your eyes

it's just like trying to the fire's inrush

it's just like falling into the mad wolf's mouth

as if you wanted to die induced in the sin of my
heart